LET'S DRAW STEP BY STEP

Let's Draw PREHISTORIC MONSTERS

KASIA DUDZIUK

WINDMILL BOOKS

Published in 2020 by Windmill Books,
an Imprint of Rosen Publishing
29 East 21st Street, New York, NY 10010

Cataloging-in-Publication Data

Names: Dudziuk, Kasia.
Title: Let's draw prehistoric monsters / Kasia Dudziuk.
Description: New York : Windmill Books, 2020. | Series: Let's draw step by step | Includes glossary and index.
Identifiers: ISBN 9781538391402 (pbk.) | ISBN 9781538391426 (library bound) | ISBN 9781538391419 (6 pack)
Subjects: LCSH: Prehistoric animals in art--Juvenile literature. | Drawing--Technique--Juvenile literature.
Classification: LCC NC780.5 D839 2019 | DDC 743.6--dc23

Manufactured in the United States of America

CPSIA Compliance Information: Batch BS19WM: For Further Information contact Rosen Publishing, New York, New York at 1-800-237-9932

Contents

Let's Draw!

Welcome to the world of drawing! In this book you'll learn how to draw all sorts of prehistoric monsters in four easy steps. All you need is a pencil and paper, and some crayons, colored pencils, or markers for coloring in.

Pteranodon

1 Begin by drawing the head and beak of your Pteranodon (teh-RAN-oh-don).

2 Then draw a pointed crest on the back of the head, and add the small body.

3 Now draw the thin arms and legs. They have claws at the ends.

4 Finish your Pteranodon with a beady eye and big wings like a bat.

Dimorphodon

1 Start with the head of your Dimorphodon (dy-MOR-foh-don). Its mouth is open wide.

2 Draw this shape for the body.

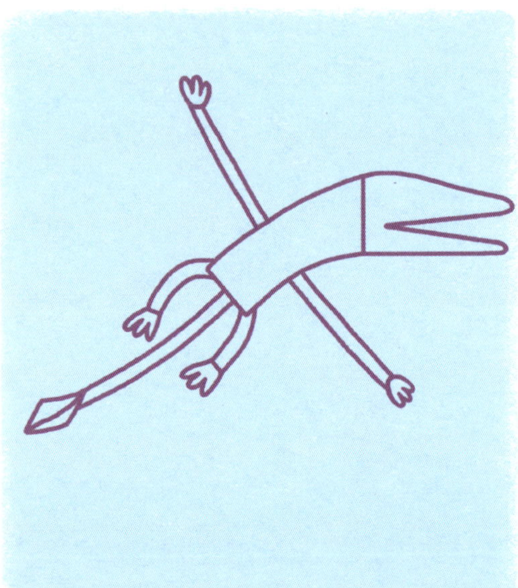

3 Now draw the two thin legs, arms, and a long tail. The tail has a diamond shape at the end.

4 Finally, add the face, some teeth, and big, green wings.

Fire! Fire! Dimorphodons could fly away with their wings made of skin.

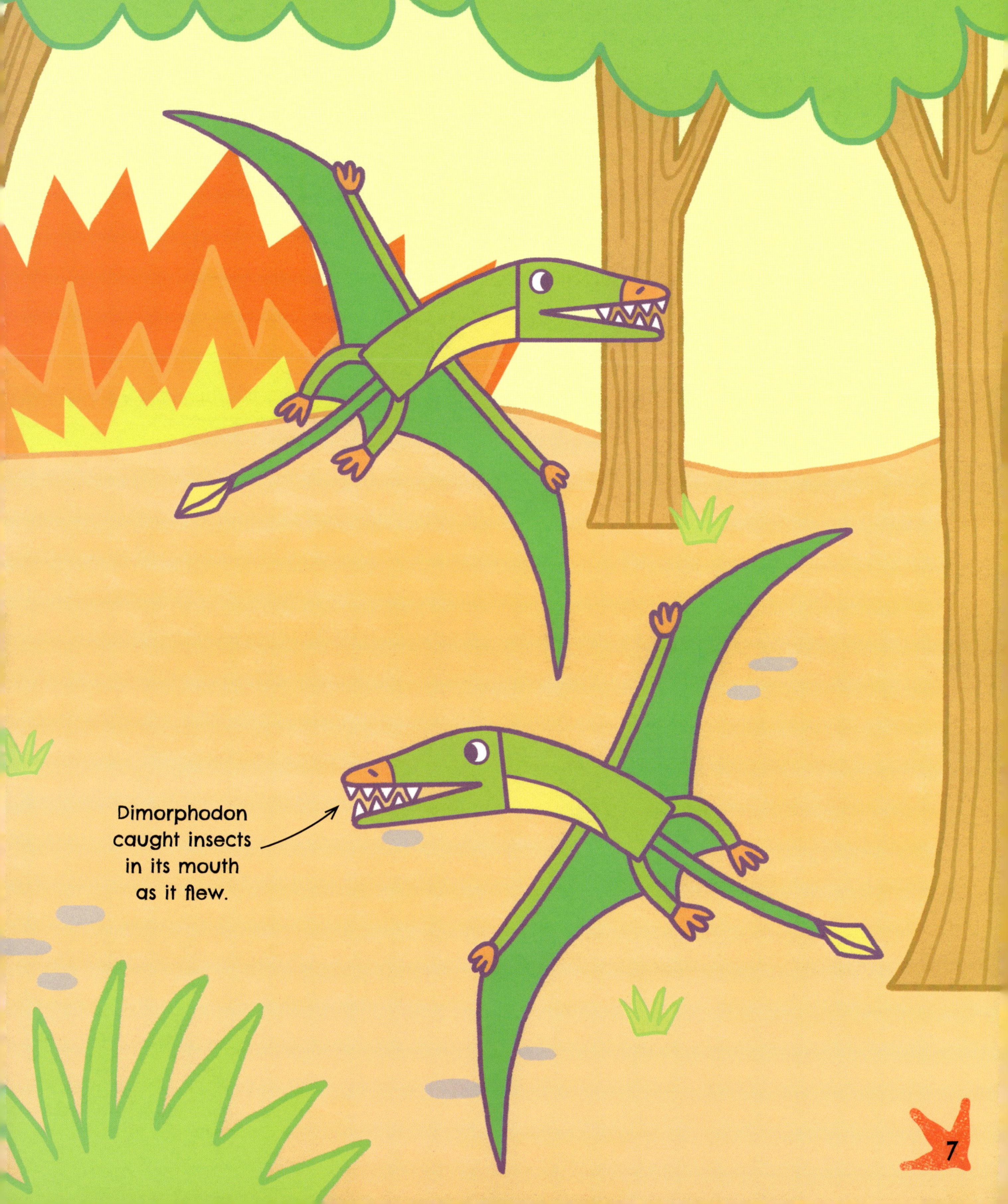

Pterodactylus

1 Draw this shape for the head of the Pterodactylus (TEH-ro-DACK-tih-lus).

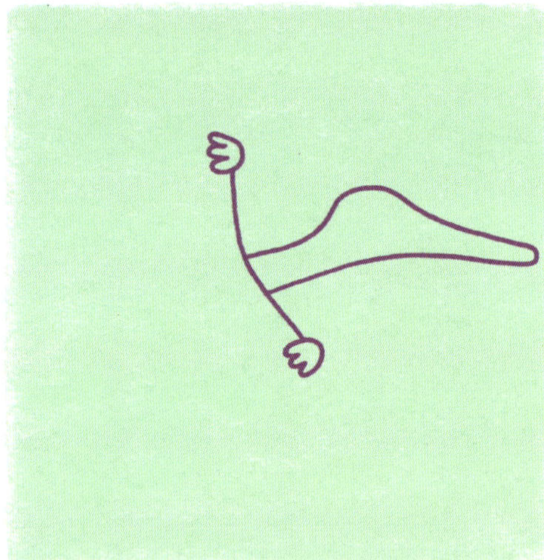

2 Then add a line for the top of the wings and add some tiny hands.

3 Draw big, sweeping wings.

4 Add the legs, face, and head crest.

Pterodactylus's name means "winged finger."

This creature loved to go fishing.

Dsungaripterus

1 First, draw the head and body of your Dsungaripterus (sun-ga-RIP-ter-us).

2 Give it long, thin arms and legs.

3 Now add the wings.

4 Add the face and lots of white teeth.

Dsungaripterus's mouth had a strange, pointed tip.

Quetzalcoatlus

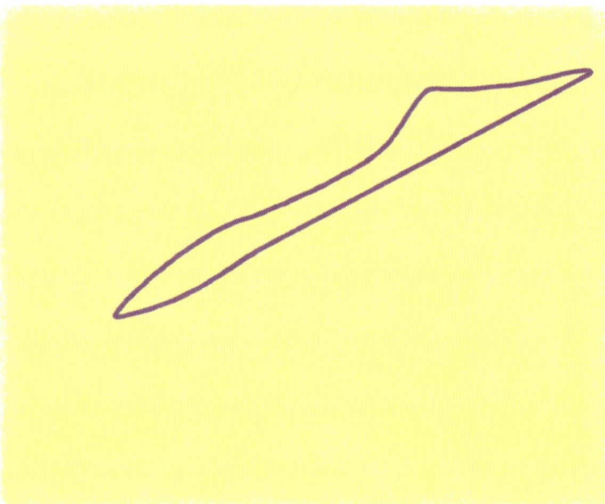

1 Let's start with the head and body of the Quetzacoatlus (KWETS-ul-koh-AT-luss).

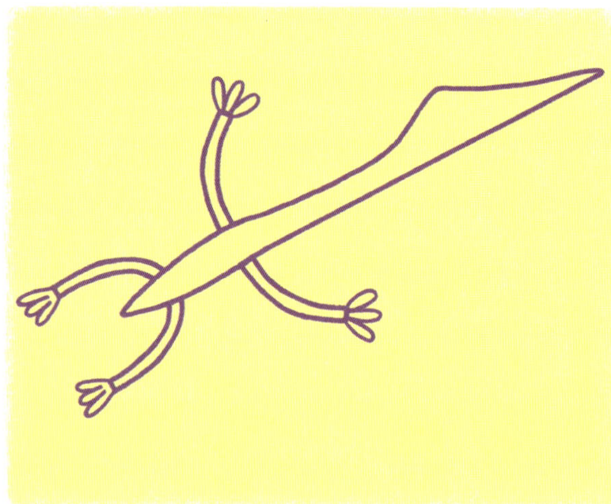

2 Add the little, skinny arms and legs.

3 Now draw the bat-like wings.

4 Draw the face and head crest to finish.

Quetzalcoatlus was the biggest flying creature the Earth has ever known.

It liked to hunt for fish.

Archaeopteryx

1 Begin with the body of your Archaeopteryx (ARK-ee-OPT-er-ix).

2 Add the feathery wings.

3 Draw a head and long neck. Add some tail feathers and legs.

4 It has a face like a bird and little red feet.

Archaeopteryx means "ancient wing."
It was the very first bird on Earth.

Plesiosaurus

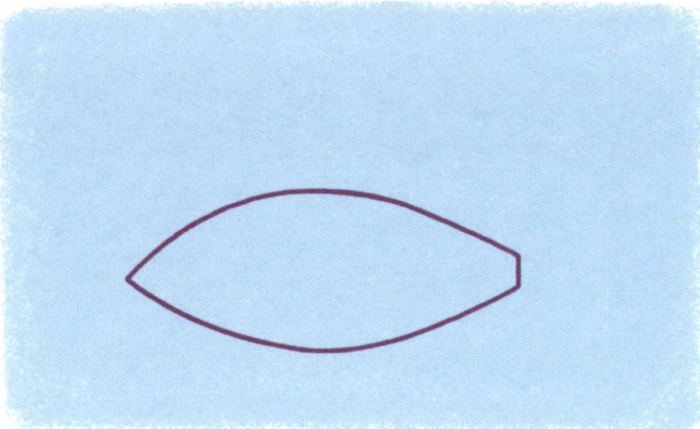

1 First, draw the body of the Plesiosaurus (PLEH-zee-oh-SORE-us).

2 Add four flippers.

3 Now draw a head and long, long neck.

4 Draw the face, a tail, and some bright stripes.

Mosasaurus

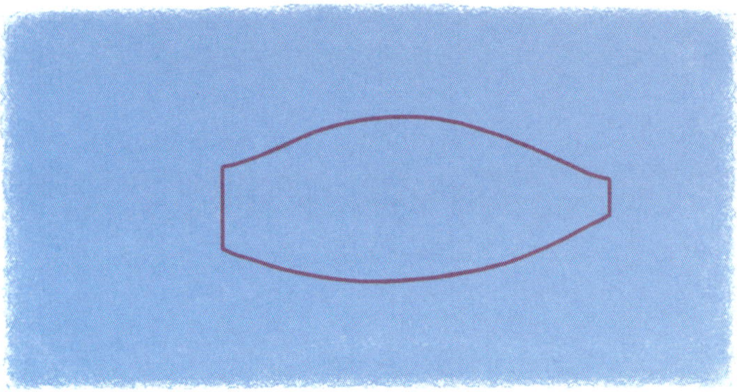

1 Start by drawing the body of your Mosasaurus (MOH-sah-SORE-us).

2 Add four pointed flippers.

3 Draw the head. It has a big mouth!

4 Add a tail fin and some sharp, white teeth to finish.

Mosasaurus was a giant sea lizard.

This creature hunted fish and turtles.

Glyptodon

1 First, draw this shape for the body of your Glyptodon (GLIP-toh-don).

2 Now add the head at the front.

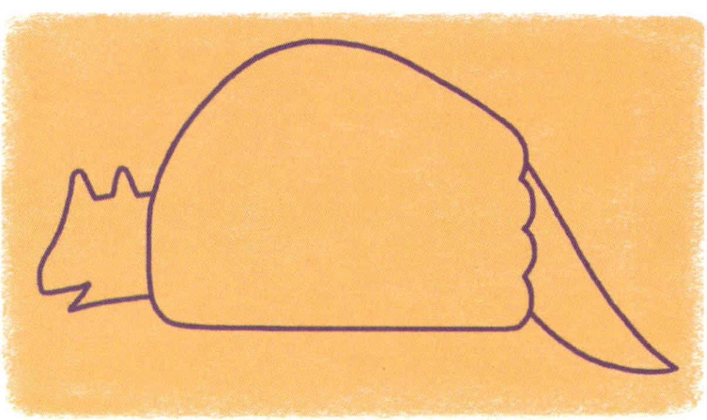

3 Draw a thick tail.

4 Add four short legs, an eye, and a nose. The body has strong plates.

Mammoth

1 First, draw the head of your mammoth (MAM-uth). It has big tusks and a long trunk!

2 Now add a big ear.

3 Draw the body and two strong legs.

4 Add the tail and the other legs. Draw an eye. Color the mammoth brown all over.

Stone Age people hunted mammoths!

They cooked the meat on fires, and used the skins for clothes and shelters.

Titanoboa

1 Start by drawing the head of your Titanoboa (ty-TAN-oh-BO-ah). This creature is a giant snake!

2 Draw the wiggly body.

3 Add a wiggly tail!

4 Draw a face and long red tongue. Add some bright green spots.

Titanoboas were monster snakes!

They hunted fish and turtles in the water.

Mastodon

1 Draw the head of your mastodon (MASS-toh-don). It has long, curly tusks.

2 Give it a big ear.

3 Draw the body. This creature looks a bit like an elephant.

4 Add four legs, an eye, and a tail.

Mastodons were early relatives of elephants.

They ate twigs, leaves, and pine needles.

Gigantopithecus

1 Start by drawing the face of your Gigantopithecus (gi-GAN-toh-PITH-ih-cus).

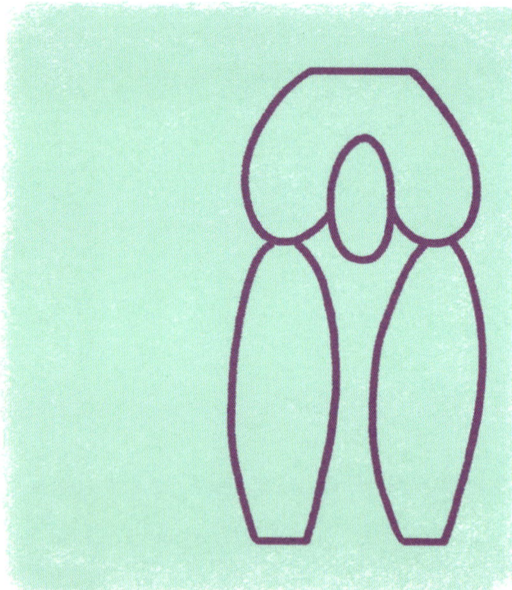

2 Now add the strong front legs.

3 Draw this shape for the body and back legs.

4 Add feet, little ears, and fur on the head. Its coat is orange and its face looks a bit angry!

Gigantopithecus's name means "giant ape."

Gigantopithecus munched on bamboo, seeds, and fruit.

Glossary

beady Small, round, and greedy looking.

beak A part of the mouth that sticks out on some animals and is used to tear food.

claws The sharp nails on the feet of animals.

crest A showy tuft or growth on the top of an animal's head.

flippers The wide, flat legs of sea creatures such as seals that are adapted for swimming.

shelters Structures that give protection from the weather.

Stone Age A very long time ago when people used stone tools.

tail feathers The feathers at the end of a bird or dinosaur.

tail fin The fin at the end of a fish.

tusks Very big teeth that stick out of the mouth when it is closed.

Further Information

Books

Cuddy, Robbin. *Learn to Draw Dinosaurs*. Lake Forest, CA: Walter Foster Jr., 2015.

Lambert, Nat. *How to Draw 101 Dinosaurs*. Woodbridge, UK: Imagine That Publishing, 2017

Legendre, Philippe. *I Can Draw! Dinosaurs, Dragons & Prehistoric Creatures*. Irvine, CA: Walter Foster Jr., 2014.

Watson, Adora L. *Learn to Draw Dinosaurs for Kids: Step-by-Step Instructions for 25 Dinosaurs*. Scotts Valley, CA: CreateSpace, 2016.

Websites

www.artforkidshub.com/how-to-draw/animals/prehistoric
This website uses videos to show you how to draw all sorts of prehistoric creatures.

www.kids-dinosaurs.com
This website has facts and activities on many prehistoric dinosaurs.

Publisher's note to educators and parents: Our editors have carefully reviewed these websites to ensure that they are suitable for students. Many websites change frequently, however, and we cannot guarantee that a site's future contents will continue to meet our high standards of quality and educational value. Be advised that students should be closely supervised whenever they access the Internet.

Index